Who Are You?

Four Temperaments

Virginia Loh-Hagan

45TH PARALLEL PRESS

Published in the United States of America by Cherry Lake Publishing Group
Ann Arbor, Michigan
www.cherrylakepublishing.com

Reading Adviser: Marla Conn, MS, Ed., Literacy specialist, Read-Ability, Inc.
Book Designer: Felicia Macheske

Photo Credits: © V.S.Anandhakrishna/Shutterstock.com, cover; © jstudio/Shutterstock.com, 5; © Sabphoto/Shutterstock.com, 6; © Heijo/Shutterstock.com, 9; © Michail Patakos/Shutterstock.com, 11; © Ermolaev Alexander/Shutterstock.com, 12; © OneStockPhoto/Shutterstock.com, 15; © Samuel Borges Photography/Shutterstock.com, 17; © Syda Productions/Shutterstock.com, 18; © Take A Pix Media/Shutterstock.com, 20; © Africa Studio/Shutterstock.com, 22; © Golden Pixels LLC/Shutterstock.com, 25; © Liyba Dozz/Shutterstock.com, 27; © yoeml/Shutterstock.com, 29; © Anton Starikov/Shutterstock.com, 31

Graphics Throughout: © AKaiser/Shutterstock.com; © galastudio/Shutterstock.com; © tanyabosyk/Shutterstock.com; © ViSnezh/Shutterstock.com; © MARINA ARABADZHI/Shutterstock.com; © Alisa Burkovska/Shutterstock.com

45th Parallel Press is an imprint of Cherry Lake Publishing Group.

Library of Congress Cataloging-in-Publication Data

Names: Loh-Hagan, Virginia, author.
Title: Four temperaments / Virginia Loh-Hagan.
Description: Ann Arbor, Michigan : Cherry Lake Publishing, [2020] | Series: Who are you? | Includes index.
Identifiers: LCCN 2020006959 (print) | LCCN 2020006960 (ebook) | ISBN 9781534169180 (hardcover) | ISBN 9781534170865 (paperback) | ISBN 9781534172708 (pdf) | ISBN 9781534174542 (ebook)
Subjects: LCSH: Four temperaments—Juvenile literature. | Personality tests—Juvenile literature.
Classification: LCC BF801 .L64 2020 (print) | LCC BF801 (ebook) | DDC 155.2/62—dc23
LC record available at https://lccn.loc.gov/2020006959
LC ebook record available at https://lccn.loc.gov/2020006960

Cherry Lake Publishing Group would like to acknowledge the work of the Partnership for 21st Century Learning, a Network of Battelle for Kids. Please visit *http://www.battelleforkids.org/networks/p21* for more information.

Printed in the United States of America
Corporate Graphics

Dr. Virginia Loh-Hagan is an author, university professor, and former classroom teacher. She took a free online quiz at https://openpsychometrics.org/tests/O4TS. She scored 19/24 on Choleric. She scored 18/24 on Sanguine. She scored 11/24 on Phlegmatic. She scored 9/24 on Melancholic. She lives in San Diego, California, with her very tall husband and very naughty dogs. To learn more about her, visit www.virginialoh.com.

Chapter One

Four Humors

What does temperament mean? What are the 4 humors? How do humors affect people's temperaments?

Temperaments means personalities. They're people's natures. They're a combination of people's traits. The Four Temperaments is a personality system. It's based on **ancient** Greek ideas. Ancient means from a long time ago.

Ancient Greeks believed the human body was filled with 4 main substances. These substances are called the "four **humors**." Humors are body liquid. The four humors are blood, yellow **bile**, black bile, and **phlegm**. Bile is a sour fluid made by the liver. Phlegm is gunk from the lungs.

The 4 humors are connected to body organs. Blood is connected to the liver. Yellow bile is connected to the spleen. Black bile is connected to the gallbladder. Phlegm is connected to the lungs and brain.

Think about a time you accidentally hurt your body. How did that affect your mood? How did you feel?

The 4 humors are also connected to the 4 life elements. Blood is connected to air. Yellow bile is connected to fire. Black bile is connected to earth. Phlegm is connected to water.

The 4 humors are also connected to the stars. They're connected to seasons. All of these things could affect people's humors. This affects people's body, mind, and soul.

When all 4 humors are balanced, people are healthy. When the 4 humors are not balanced, people are unhealthy. Having too much or too little is bad. Diet could affect the balance. Exercise could affect the balance. Air quality could affect the balance. The key is to have a balanced life.

It's important to eat healthy foods.
Do you eat a balanced diet?

FUN FACTS

* Carl Philipp Emanuel Bach lived from 1714 to 1788. He was the son of Johann Sebastian Bach, the famous composer. Composers write music. Carl wrote a song about the Four Temperaments. It's called "Sanguineus et Melancholicus."

* Carl Nielsen lived from 1865 to 1931. He was a Danish musician. He wrote a song called "De Fire Temperamenter." He was inspired when he saw a funny picture of the Four Temperaments.

* Ancient doctors cut people. They did this to let the blood out. They wanted to get rid of humors.

* William Shakespeare lived from 1564 to 1616. He was a famous writer. He referred to humors often. For example, he wrote, "I beseech you, be not so phlegmatic."

* Queen Elizabeth I ruled England from 1558 to 1603. During this time, people balanced humors with food and drinks. Sick people coughed up phlegm. They drank wine to balance the humors. Wine was a choleric drink.

There are 4 main temperaments. They're based on the 4 humors.

- **Sanguine:** Sanguine means positive. This type is connected to blood.
- **Choleric:** Choleric means grumpy. This type is connected to yellow bile.
- **Melancholic:** Melancholic means sad. This type is connected to black bile.
- **Phlegmatic:** Phlegmatic means calm. This type is connected to phlegm.

Most people have a **dominant** type. Dominant means main. This means people are mostly a single type. Some people may have 2 dominant types. Some people can be a mixture of different types. They can also change types. Each temperament describes how people act and feel about events.

Think about how you react to problems.
What is your dominant temperament?

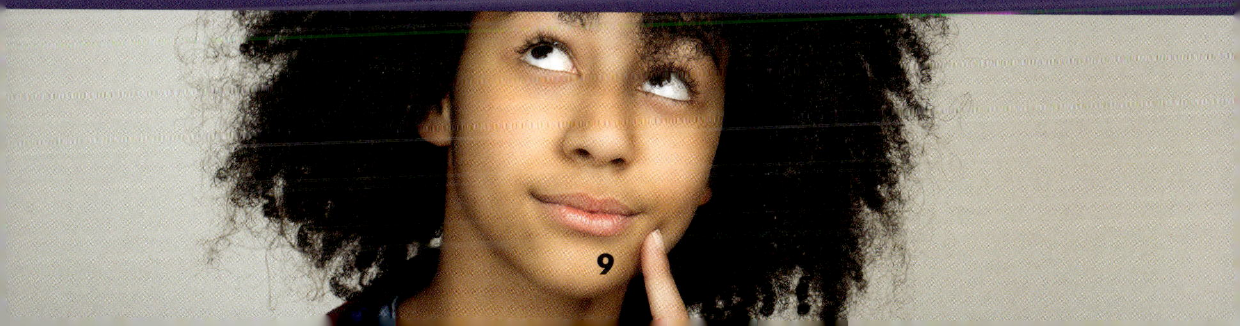

Chapter Two

Greek Roots

Who is Hippocrates? Who is Galen? What is the influence of the Four Temperaments?

Hippocrates was an ancient Greek doctor. He's called the Father of Medicine. He was one of the first to create a system about sicknesses and health. His ideas led to the Four Temperaments. He may have been inspired by the ancient Egyptians and ancient Mesopotamians. Today, Mesopotamia is Iran.

Hippocrates was also inspired by Alcmaeon of Croton. Alcmaeon was an ancient Greek doctor. He was the first to connect humors to the way people live.

Hippocrates connected humors to sickness. He said humors caused a body's "pains and health." He believed the mind and body acted as a single unit. So, sicknesses were caused by both mind and body.

Do you know the Hippocratic oath?
Look it up. Why is it important?

Galen was an ancient Greek doctor. He was inspired by Hippocrates. He wrote about Hippocrates's ideas about humors. He helped make them popular. He added the idea of balance. He said people had different levels of humors. He connected this balance to temperaments. He came up with the names of the temperaments.

Hippocrates's and Galen's ideas developed the ancient medical concept of **humorism**. Humorism is the idea that humors affect people's traits and behaviors.

Ancient Greeks believed humors caused sicknesses. Sicknesses were combinations of hot and cold or wet and dry. Blood caused hot and wet sicknesses. Yellow bile caused hot and dry sicknesses. Black bile caused cold and dry sicknesses. Phlegm caused cold and wet sicknesses.

Think about the last time you were sick.
In what ways were you hot, cold, wet, or dry?

EXPLAINED BY
SCIENCE

Phlegm looks like a pile of snot. It's important. It traps bad things from the air. It clears these bad things out of the body. There are 2 ways to get rid of phlegm. First, it can be coughed up. Second, it can be swallowed. Stomach acids will process the phlegm. Phlegm will be pooped out. Once it's out of the body, phlegm is called sputum. It has different colors. Colors range from clear to dark gray. Yellow or green means sickness. Clear means allergies. Phlegm is made from mucus. Mucus is the wet lining inside of people. It's a protective layer. It lines airways. It lines eyes. It lines noses. It lines stomachs and other organs. It's mainly water. Phlegm is not mucus. But phlegm has mucus. It also has bad germs and other cells.

Ancient Greek doctors cured sicknesses using humorist ideas. They had people eat and drink things to balance the humors. For example, warm foods made yellow bile. Cold foods made phlegm. Ancient Greek doctors made people throw up. These doctors cut people to let their blood flow out. This was how the doctors made sure treatments were working.

Ancient Roman and Islamic doctors also practiced humorism. This idea lasted until the 1900s. Modern doctors learned more about sicknesses. They separated the mind and body. They found that sicknesses had specific causes.

The theory of the Four Temperaments is no longer a part of medical science. But it's still popular. It inspired many of today's personality tests. For example, it inspired the Myers-Briggs test.

Read the 45th Parallel Press book about Myers-Briggs. How is it connected to the Four Temperaments?

Chapter Three

Humor Types

What are the strengths and weaknesses of each temperament?

Too much blood leads to a sanguine temperament. Sanguine people are social. They talk a lot. They have a lot of energy. They like being part of a crowd. They're **extroverted**. Extroverted means outgoing. Sanguine personality types are active. They have a hard time doing nothing. They enjoy being busy. They always have a ton of ideas.

Sanguine personality types have weaknesses. They may take too many risks. They can do unsafe things. They react very quickly. They act before they think. They have strong feelings. They have short attention spans. They get distracted easily. They have a hard time finishing projects.

Sanguine types are a lot of fun.
How are you like a sanguine temperament?

Too much yellow bile leads to a choleric temperament. Choleric people are extroverted too. They're independent. They can figure out things on their own. They're good at making decisions. They work toward their goals. They make things happen. They want to be successful. They get people to listen to them. They take charge.

Choleric personality types have weaknesses. They're **aggressive**. Aggressive means they're likely to attack. These types can be violent. They have short tempers. They hold grudges for a long time. They tend to care more about winning than feelings. They can push people too far. They're not patient. They can be too controlling.

Choleric types are good leaders.
How are you like a choleric temperament?

Too much black bile leads to a melancholic temperament. Melancholic people are thinkers. They feel things deeply. They like learning. They read a lot. They research. They're logical. They pay attention to details. They work hard until things are done right. They're very neat. They support others. They don't like getting a lot of attention. They're **introverted**. Introverted means shy.

Melancholic personality types have weaknesses. They can be anxious. They're nervous. They're fearful. They take a long time to make decisions. They like things to be perfect. This means they can get too picky.

Melancholic types are good learners.
How are you like a melancholic temperament?

REAL-LIFE

CONNECTION

The New York City Ballet created a ballet called *The Four Temperaments*. It's about the 4 humors. It was first performed in 1944. The music was written by Paul Hindemith. Hindemith was a famous German composer. He fled the Nazis. He taught music at Yale. George Balanchine was called the Father of American Ballet. He founded and led the New York City Ballet. He created the dance moves. He said *The Four Temperaments* is an "expression in dance and music of the ancient notion that the human organism is made up of four different humors, or temperaments." The titles of the ballet's 4 movements are "Melancholic," "Sanguinic," "Phlegmatic," and "Choleric." Each movement represents the mood of each temperament. In the last scene, 4 ballerinas leap offstage. The ballet is thought to be a creation story. It's still performed today.

Too much phlegm leads to a phlegmatic temperament. Phlegmatic people are introverted. But they're also social. They care deeply about others. They want people to be happy. They don't like fighting. They're peaceful. They're calm. They're relaxed. They're easy to get along with. They make friends easily. They make **compromises**. Compromises are deals where everyone wins.

Phlegmatic personality types have weaknesses. They hide their true feelings. They take a long time to do things. They lose interest quickly. They react slowly. They're hard to inspire. They can be **apathetic**. Apathetic means showing no interest.

Phlegmatic types are team players.
How are you like a phlegmatic temperament?

Chapter Four

Famous Examples

How is Elvis Presley sanguine? How is Margaret Thatcher choleric? How is Beethoven melancholic? How is Thomas Aquinas phlegmatic?

Elvis Presley lived from 1935 to 1977. He's called the "King of Rock and Roll." He sang many hit songs. He starred in many popular movies. He performed in many concerts. Presley was a sanguine type. He was fun and charming. He had a great sense of humor. He was loved by many people. He has many fans and fan clubs. Every year, fans celebrate Elvis Week.

Margaret Thatcher was a choleric type. She lived from 1925 to 2013. She was the prime minister of the United Kingdom. She served from 1979 to 1990. She was the first woman to hold that position. She was called the Iron Lady. She was a strong leader. She was tough.

Think about your family members.
How would you describe their temperaments?

Ludwig van Beethoven lived from 1770 to 1827. He was a German pianist and composer. Beethoven is one of the greatest musical talents of all time.

He struggled his whole life. He was very shy. He never married. He didn't have children. His brother died. He was lonely. He got mad easily. He thought people were out to get him. He fought with everybody. He was going deaf. He wrote, "I must confess that I lead a miserable life." He was a melancholic type. He even wrote melancholic songs.

Listen to a Beethoven song.

What do you think? Can you feel his melancholy?

SPOTLIGHT

BIOGRAPHY

Dr. Helen E. Fisher studies human relationships. She studies people's brains. She took pictures of brains at different stages of love. She used brain science to create her own personality test. Her test is called the Helen Fisher's Personality Quiz. Fisher's test has 56 questions. It's used on dating sites. It helps people find their matches. Over 14 million people have taken her test. Fisher linked 4 brain systems to personalities. The brain systems are dopamine, serotonin, testosterone, and estrogen. Humans have all 4 systems. But they have different levels. These levels create different personalities, or temperaments. Fisher's 4 temperaments are Explorer (dopamine), Negotiator (estrogen), Director (testosterone), and Builder (serotonin). Fisher's types are very similar to the Four Temperaments. Explorer is similar to sanguine. Negotiator is similar to phlegmatic. Director is similar to choleric. Builder is similar to melancholic.

Thomas Aquinas lived from 1225 to 1274. He was an Italian philosopher and a Catholic priest. He is a **saint**. Saints are holy people. He combined faith and reason. He wrote many texts. He traveled. He taught. He persuaded people to follow him. People liked his peaceful personality. They were impressed by his great learning. Aquinas was called The **Universal** Teacher. Universal refers to everyone.

Aquinas was a phlegmatic type. He was careful with his words. He was very thoughtful. He used common sense. He was gentle. He cared about people. He said, "There is nothing on this earth more to be prized than true friendship."

Some people think Jesus Christ embodies all 4 temperaments. Do you agree or disagree?

WHO ARE YOU?

TAKE THE QUIZ!

What would you do at a party? Your temperament tends to come out at parties.

- You dance. You make jokes. You laugh loudly. You move around from room to room. You're the life of a party. **You're sanguine.**
- You host the party. You tell everyone to come. You lead the party games. You're a natural leader. **You're choleric.**
- You plan the party. You decorate. You like to sit in a single place. You like to watch everyone. You're the perfectionist. **You're melancholic.**
- You make sure everyone is having fun. You talk to everyone. You make sure there's no drama. You're the peacemaker. **You're phlegmatic.**

Which career fields are you interested in? Knowing your temperament could help you plan for the future.

- Art, Entertainment, Fashion, or Sports: **You're sanguine.**
- Business, Science, or Technology: **You're choleric.**
- Accounting, Management, or Social Work: **You're melancholic.**
- Healthcare, Nonprofit, or Teaching: **You're phlegmatic**.

DISCLAIMER: All the quizzes and questions in this book are designed for entertainment purposes only. They shouldn't be used as advice. They shouldn't be taken seriously. There is no guarantee of accuracy. But they're fun! To download a copy of this quiz, please visit: https://cherrylakepublishing.com/teaching_guides.

Which season is your favorite? Ancient Greeks paired temperaments with seasons.

- Spring: **You're sanguine.**
- Summer: **You're choleric.**
- Autumn: **You're melancholic.**
- Winter: **You're phlegmatic.**

What type of student are you? How you work is part of your temperament.

- You get excited about new projects. But you need checklists to get your work done. **You're sanguine.**
- You take over group projects. You get all your work done before the due date. **You're choleric.**
- You do top-quality work. You proofread before turning anything in. **You're melancholic.**
- You turn in a lot of work late. Sometimes you don't do your work. You do your best work in groups. **You're phlegmatic.**

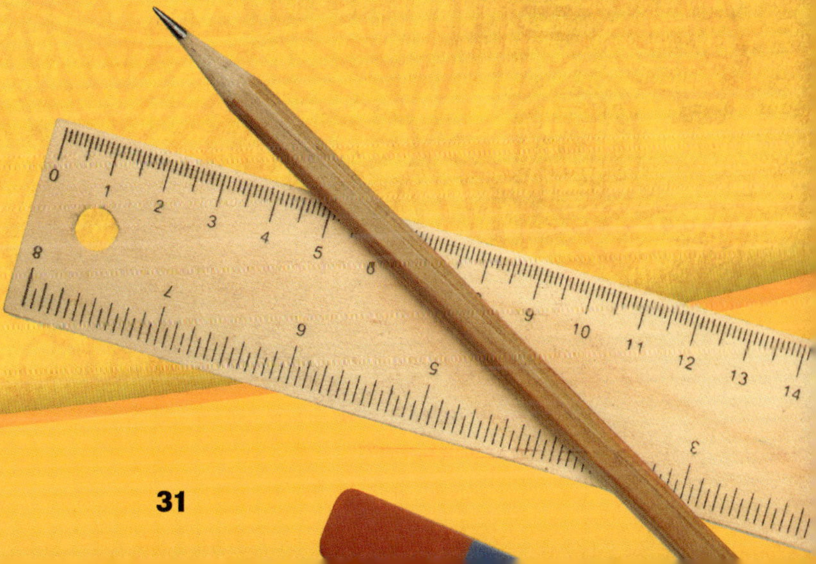

Glossary

aggressive (uh-GRES-iv) prone to being violent, hostile

ancient (AYN-shuhnt) from a time long ago

apathetic (ap-uh-THET-ik) showing no interest

bile (BILE) fluid made by the liver

choleric (KAL-uh-rik) grumpy

compromises (KAHM-pruh-mize-iz) win-win deals

dominant (DAH-muh-nuhnt) main

extroverted (EK-struh-vurt-id) outgoing

humorism (HYOO-mur-ih-zum) ancient medical concept that humors affect people's personalities

humors (HYOO-murz) body fluids

introverted (IN-truh-vurt-id) shy

melancholic (MEL-uhn-kah-lik) sad

phlegm (FLEM) liquid gunk from lungs

phlegmatic (FLEG-mah-tik) calm

saint (SAYNT) holy person

sanguine (SANG-win) positive

temperaments (TEM-pur-uh-muhnts) personalities

universal (yoo-nuh-VUR-suhl) belonging to everyone

Index